W9-ATB-103

CONTAINER GARDENING
for Kids

Ellen Talmage

Photographed by Bruce Curtis

Sterling Publishing Co., Inc.
New York

This book is lovingly dedicated to Mom

*Sunshine and water let plants grow, but children
thrive on your love and kindness*

Edited by Claire Bazinet
Designed by Judy Morgan

Library of Congress Cataloging-in-Publication Data

Talmage, Ellen.
    Container gardening for kids / by Ellen Talmage;
photographed by Bruce Curtis.
        p.   cm.
    Includes index.
    Summary: Provides instructions for propagating and caring for
plants, with more than twenty beginning gardening projects.
    ISBN 0-8069-1378-9
    1. Container gardening—Juvenile literature.   2. Nature craft—
Juvenile literature.   [1. Container gardening.   2. Indoor
gardening.]   I. Curtis, Bruce, ill.   II. Title.
SB418.T335   1995
635'.048—dc20   95-49197
                                                                    CIP
                                                                    AC

1 3 5 7 9 8 6 4 2

Published by Sterling Publishing Company, Inc.
387 Park Avenue South, New York, N.Y. 10016
© 1996 by Ellen Talmage
Distributed in Canada by Sterling Publishing
℅ Canadian Manda Group, One Atlantic Avenue, Suite 105
Toronto, Ontario, Canada M6K 3E7
Distributed in Great Britain and Europe by Cassell PLC
Wellington House, 125 Strand, London WC2R 0BB, England
Distributed in Australia by Capricorn Link (Australia) Pty Ltd.
P.O. Box 6651, Baulkham Hills, Business Centre, NSW 2153, Australia
Printed in Hong Kong

Sterling ISBN 0-8069-1378-9

Contents

Introduction 4

Growing Basics 5

Projects:

A Tisket, a Tasket…A Garden in a Basket 8
I Don't Play with That Anymore 11
Ring a Round of Ivy 14
Sshhhh! Here Come the Butterflies! 16
Tiny Gardens for Giant Fun 18

Making Baby Plants—the Fine Art of Propagation 20

Starting Seeds–Rooting a Leaf–Rooting Tip
Cuttings–Divide and Conquer

More Projects:

A Fungus Amongus! 26
The Tough Get Growing 28
Is It Spring Yet? 30
Tiptoe Through the Tulips 33

Gardens on Parade 36
Herbs for the Furry Set 37
Personality Pots 40
Potato Pals 42
Summer Party Centerpiece 44
Strawflowers—from Seed to Craft 46
Pumpkin Pots for Everyone 49
That Monster Tomato Needs a Cage! 51
Salad on a Stick 54
Petunia Pig 56
Triple-Treat Garden 59
Time for a Sundial Garden 61
Grow an Herb Pillow 63
Happy Holidays Winter Garden 66

Plants to Know and Grow 68

Notes About Supplies 77

Glossary 78

Index 79

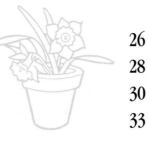

Introduction

Planting small gardens in containers is fun and easy. All garden plants have things in common.

* They all need light to help them make their food.
* They all need water for their roots to drink.
* They all need some soil to keep the roots dark and protected.
* They all need fertilizer to give them healthy green leaves.

As you will see, plants can differ a lot from each other just like people can. Try to pick the best plants to do the job you want them to do. The beauty and fun of gardening is to experiment. If you combine many colors and varieties of plant, keep in mind that their requirements should be the same. In other words, plants go into the same container if they all need the same amount of light, water, soil, and fertilizer. It's not that hard, you will see! And remember, if at first you don't succeed, plant, plant again!

It is important to know that no gardener has complete success. Because you are dealing with Mother Nature, you should expect a certain amount of disappointment. Keep a notebook handy to write down what you do and when, and record your successes and failures. Sometimes, the best way to learn to grow a kind of plant is to kill it first. You will seldom make the same mistake twice.

Don't get discouraged. Eventually, your many successes will outweigh your failures.

Growing Basics

* Container gardening requires few tools. With in-ground gardening, you will often need a hoe, shovel, rake, wheelbarrow, pruning shears, garden hose, protective gloves, etc. Container gardening can be enjoyed with the help of just a few common household items (spoons and maybe a trowel, scissors, sharp knife, watering can and spray bottle, notebook and pencil) and some gardening supplies such as potting soil and fertilizer. For specific items, see "What You Need" in each project.

* Container gardens make great gifts. As you create living works of art, you are certain to think of friends and family who would enjoy them. Unlike cut flowers, which look nice for only a short time, container gardens can bring pleasure for months!

Choosing Plants

Plants are often sold based on pot size. Young plants, sold in market packs (4, 6, or 8 pockets) or small, 2 inch (5 cm) pots are usually cheaper than those in

There are real advantages to planting in containers rather than in the ground.
* Container gardening allows you to garden year-round. You can easily move the gardens inside if the weather gets too cold.
* Container gardening doesn't require a lot of space. Even if you live in the city, you can always find room for some green friends.
* Container gardening lets you be creative. There are endless possibilities of containers to use and plants to plant in them.

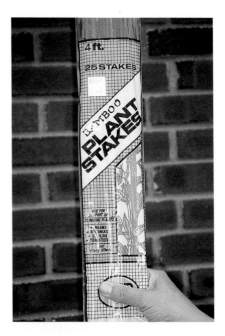

(If you need to get the soil just right, for a large garden or an expensive plant, it might be worth having the soil tested.) Limestone is very inexpensive and easy to find in most hardware and garden stores. Adding it will help the root system absorb the nutrients a plant needs.

larger pots which are more developed. The size plants needed for projects in this book may be referred to by pot size.

How Sweet It Is

Most gardening plants thrive in a slightly acid to neutral soil. Commercial potting soils are adjusted to be just right, so that plants can absorb all the nutrients they need.

If the same potting soil has been reused through several growing seasons, however, you may want to put in additional fertilizer and some calcium to "sweeten the soil." The amount of calcium, in the form of limestone, to add will depend on how acid your soil is.

Providing Support

If you experiment with taller plants in your gardens, or have droopy ones, regardless of their height, you will probably want to do some staking. Providing such plants with support will help them stand straighter and not fall over (think of the stake as a walking cane). Strong, green-colored gardening

stakes are available in all sizes at most garden centers, or regular sticks can be used.

Tall plants can be staked about 3 weeks after planting them in their final pots. The stake should be at least half the expected height of the flower when in full bloom—in other words, if a plant will be 4 feet (120 cm) tall when it flowers, the stake should reach 2 feet (60 cm) or higher above the soil line. Large twist or other ties can be used to fix tall or drooping stems to a stake. Place one or several "bracelets" around the stake and stem, but make them loose so they do not choke the plant.

Pruning

Outdoor shrubs or trees are usually pruned to remove diseased or dead branches and flowers. In container gardening, pruning is mostly done to make plants grow full and bushy. Look for long lanky stems that have lost most of their bottom leaves and have faded flower heads. Cut them back half the length of their stems. Removing old stems will spur new growth. Soon side shoots will appear and will fill in the plant nicely.

A Tisket, a Tasket...A Garden in a Basket

Although little plastic flowerpots are containers too, it's much more fun to use your imagination and come up with interesting new places for green and flowering plants. Baskets come in so many shapes and sizes, let's start there.

What You Need

Empty basket (old or new)

Heavy plastic bag to fit basket

8

Scissors

3 to 7 plants in small pots (however many will fit)

Prop-up material: wood blocks, cans, etc.

Mulch (sphagnum moss or finely shredded newspaper)

What You Do

Place the bag inside the basket and open it up. Trim off or fold in,

between the bag and the basket, the extra plastic around the top so that it comes only to the rim of the basket. By lining the basket in this way, you will be able to keep it in good shape and can use it again the next gardening season.

The question now is, where to keep your basket garden? If you want to put it outside, in a very sunny and perhaps windy location, you need to select plants that can tolerate strong light. You will also want to give some thought to how often your garden will have to be watered. You need to consider the different light and water needs of the plants before deciding which ones to use and combine.

When you've made your selection, remember to give each plant a good drink and clean them up, removing yellow and dead leaves, before placing them in the basket.

Arrange your plants so the tops of the pots are level with the top of the basket, or slightly below. This

Besides water and light, most plants require fertilizer in their soil to ensure healthy green leaves. Soil has many nutrients in it but, over time, water flow washes some of the "good stuff" out of the bottom of the pot. Providing container gardens with fertilizer is like having a glass of milk and a vitamin pill each day. Your plants will stay their healthiest if they receive all the nutrients they require.

Fertilizing plants is something that can be done every second or third week. There are many types and forms of fertilizer. Ask an adult to help you choose what will work best. A liquid fertilizer or one that dissolves in water seems to be the easiest to find and use. Just follow the directions on the bottle or package. Mark the dates you add fertilizer—an "F" will do—in your notebook or calendar. Be sure to give the new garden at least two regular waterings, to get it settled in, before you start fertilizing. Remember, you *can* have too much of a good thing. Fertilizing at too high a strength, or too often, can actually hurt a plant.

part may be a little tricky, depending on the depth of the basket. Remember, anything goes. Search around for blocks of wood, empty soda or other cans, stones, or broken bricks. You can use anything you want to prop your pots up to the basket rim. (Think of it as holding up little kids to see over a fence.) The pots should look level and as if the plants have been growing together in the

9

basket all along. (No one will know your "little kids" secret but you.)

Put sphagnum moss or shredded newspaper, as mulch, on top of the basket. Mulch keeps the soil from drying out too quickly and, in this case, hides the pot rims, bringing your garden together.

Move or change the pots and plants as often or as little as you like. Care for the basket garden as you would any potted plant.

When to Water

Knowing when a plant needs water is a skill that takes practice. For starters, keep these general rules in mind:

* Outdoor plants in a sunny and windy location need water once a day.
* Outdoor plants in a sunny place protected from the wind need water every other day.
* Outdoor plants in shady places need water every third day.
* Indoor plants need to be watered every fourth day.

Sure, it's a help to follow the above guide, but how do you *really* know if your container garden needs water? The best way is to stick your finger down deep into the soil. If the soil at your fingertips feels dry, it's probably time to water. But remember, all plants do not require the same amount of water. Cactus, for instance, likes its soil really dry. You can check into the water requirements of different plants at your local garden center or library.

I Don't Play with That Anymore

Think of all the old stuff you have in your toy chest or around your room that you never use anymore. Why not recycle them as containers for your gardens?

What You Need

Great imagination

Old toy, such as football helmet, dump truck, beach pail, doll baby carriage, boat, wagon

Lots of colorful plants

Potting soil

Drainage makers (optional)

What You Do

Anything can become a garden container . . . well, anything that can hold soil (not hulahoops). When choosing old toys as planters, there are two questions to ask yourself.

First, is it O.K. to use it? The soil or "dirt" and water you put in will likely damage the container, so the best ones to consider are toys about to be thrown out. Even if you, or a sister or brother, are willing to part with something, it's best to ask a parent. A still-good toy may serve a better purpose, such as being given to a charity collection or a needy family.

Second, how long do I want this project to last? If you only want a short-term garden (to look good for a week, over a holiday, or as a party centerpiece), you don't need to worry about putting in drainage.

For gardening all season long, you need to select a container that will allow water to drain away from the roots. Sometimes, this can be done by making small openings (an adult can drill some holes) in the bottom of the toy you want to use. If that is not possible, don't give up. There's another way!

Gather up some large pebbles the size of marbles, or you could even use marbles! You can also use plastic foam peanuts, or the bubble

Tip The more you garden, the more aware you will be of each plant's bloom time. You want the garden to always look nice. Unfortunately, no plant blooms forever. To get around this, look for plants, such as coleus, that have pretty leaves instead of flowers. Then your container gardens will look great even if some plants are out of bloom.

roots will die off—and dying roots equal dying plants.

Fill your toy container with potting soil. Select colorful plants that make you happy. Sometimes growing all of one kind of plant in a toy garden increases the chance of success. Grouping all the same variety of plant in one container helps because the water, sun, and fertilizer requirements are the same!

pack that often comes in shipping boxes. (Punch lots of holes through the bubble pack with a large nail or sharp pencil so air and water can circulate.)

Line the bottom of the toy with the "drainage maker" of your choice. This makes some open spaces under the soil and gives extra water a place to go, away from the roots. Although plant roots need water, they also need air to breathe and you have to be careful not to "drown" them. Healthy soil contains space for both water and air. When too much water takes over the air spaces, the

12

How about an old dump truck as a container? You will soon notice a problem. A dump truck has only three sides so it will need help, on the fourth side, holding in the soil. Here is where a brick or a block of wood works very well.

Turn Off the Water!

O.K., so you know how to tell if something needs water. But what do you do if you've given a garden too much water, or find an outdoor garden "swimming" with rainwater? Gently, tip the container and pour off the excess water. Just as important as checking for extreme dryness is to check for extreme wetness. As in eating out, here, too, tipping is very appropriate!

Ring a Round of Ivy

What You Need

Ivy plant, 4-inch-pot size

Garden clippers or scissors

Wire coat hanger

Large-size plastic pot

Potting soil

Garbage bag twist ties

Seasonal ornament (optional)

What You Do

The plant needed for this project can either be bought in a small (4 in/10 cm) pot or you could grow it yourself. To learn how to grow a plant from a stem cutting, see the section on propagation, "Making Baby Plants." It may take up to a year to get an ivy plant with stems long enough, about 6–8 inches (36–48 cm), but growing ivy is easy. Training is, too. All you need to do is be patient and give it some T.L.C. (tender loving care).

Bend a wire hanger into a circle. Try to make it really round. If the hanger wire is too heavy and hard to shape, rest before trying again or ask someone for help. You also need to straighten the hook.

Fill a large plastic pot halfway with potting soil. You need a hole in the middle of the pot large enough to hold the ivy's roots.

Pick up the small pot of ivy and put your fingers on both sides of the stem to catch the root ball. Turn the pot over and tap it

against the edge of the bigger pot. This is the best way to remove a plant from a pot without damaging the plant's roots or stems.

Place the root ball in the large pot so that the plant is at the same soil-line level as it was in the smaller pot. Add or remove some soil underneath if it is too low or high in the pot. Gently pack more potting soil in around the roots, filling to 1 inch (2 cm) from rim.

ring as you would any other houseplant. You may have to trim off other shoots, give your ivy more "haircuts" as the plant matures. (If you root the ivy trimmings, your friends will be able to make

ivy rings, too!) Your ring will probably live happily in this size pot for a few years. When it gets too large, you can transplant it into an even larger pot.

An ivy ring can be a great seasonal decoration. Celebrate a special time of year by hanging stars, hearts, or other holiday ornaments inside the ring. Dressed up or not, ivy rings make great gifts, too!

Plunge the straightened hook of the coat hanger into the root ball of the ivy plant.

Select *two* of the longest, healthiest ivy shoots. With scissors, trim off the other shoots next to the soil line. Gently wind the two selected shoots around the wire.

Check on the plant two or three times a week to make sure the stems are still in place. If needed, use twist ties to secure the shoots to the wire ring. Once the ivy is growing happily on the ring, remove the ties so they do not choke the plant.

Water and fertilize your ivy

Room to Grow

As you shop for potted plants, you will soon discover that the bigger the pot, the bigger the price tag. Why not save your pennies, dimes, and dollars, and try to grow as many plants as you can from cuttings or small starter pots. Most healthy 2-inch (5 cm) potted plants will grow to a 4-inch (10 cm) pot size in 3–6 months, and then to 6-inch (15 cm)-size plants in 6 months to a year. Catch on? With patience and care, you can save money, and you'll learn a lot in the process.

Sshhhh! Here Come the Butterflies!

Butterflies are one of nature's finest gifts. Unfortunately, butterflies live only a few short months during the summer. By winter, they are gone. You can make more of their short stay by planting a special garden that will bring them to your door.

What You Need

Large pot, box, tub, or other container

Potting soil

Fertilizer

Butterfly-attracting plants

What You Do

To attract butterflies, you need to choose flowering plants that they especially like (a few are listed here). You can find information on other flowers that provide food for butterflies at your local library.

When choosing your plants, check to see if they are annuals (bloom all growing season) or perennials (bloom only a short time each year). If you plant perennials, the plants will need to be placed in larger pots. Perennials will continue to grow after the season is over and will flower again the following year, so they will need the extra room. Most

butterfly plants, annual or perennial, can be started from seed in the late winter or early spring.

Transplant and care for your "butterfly garden" as you would any other. Butterflies are found everywhere, all over the world, so you have a great chance of attracting them to your backyard. Just provide the kind of garden flowers they like, full sun, and protection from the wind.

A Sip of Nature

The reason butterflies come to your garden flowers is to drink the nectar. A butterfly's mouth, called a proboscis, is shaped like a long straw that curls up while the butterfly is in flight. This special mouth can fit way down inside the flower where the nectar is found. While the butterfly drinks, the flower's tiny pollen grains stick to the butterfly's body and are carried to other flowers. This process, called pollination, is how flowers reproduce, starting new plants.

Butterfly-Attracting Plants

Annuals

Cosmos *(Cosmos)*

Salvia *(Salvia)*

Vinca *(Catharanthus)*

Zinnia *(Zinnia)*

Salvia

Zinnia

Perennials

Yarrow *(Achillea)*

Coreopsis *(Coreopsis)*

Purple Coneflower *(Echinacea)*

Liatris *(Liatris)*

Phlox *(Phlox)*

Purple Coneflower

Yarrow

Tip Butterflies usually visit on sunny, windless days and don't seem to mind movement nearby. If you get close, and list in a notebook the markings of the butterflies you see, it might to fun to go to the library later and identify your visitors.

Tiny Gardens for Giant Fun

Mini-Impatiens

Irish Moss

Serissa

Foxtail

Baby's Tears

Myrtle

Aloe

Jade tree

Who says that bigger is better? Making up tiny gardens can be giant fun!

What You Need

Tiny flowerpots

Some potting soil

Small stones, for drainage

Sharp knife

Miniature plants, such as:
   Mini-Impatiens (Impatiens)
   Serissa (Serissa)
   Baby's Tears (Soleirolia)
   Aloe (Aloe)
   Irish Moss (Selaginella)
   Foxtail (Alopecurus)
   Myrtle (Myrtus)
   Jade tree (Crassula)

What You Do

Remove the plants from their pots. Cut the plants in half, dividing them in the center of the crown (where the plant comes out of the soil). Always use a sharp knife so that the cuts are clean; you are the surgeon. Clean cuts will mean less damage and stress to the plant

during the operation, but take care handling the knife so you won't hurt yourself.

Next, you need to be a barber. Root pruning is the key to success for tiny gardens. Don't be afraid to give haircuts below ground too. Balancing the amount of top growth to root growth will make mini-plants more comfortable in their tight quarters.

Place the small plants, with soil and drainage if needed, into tiny pots. Add water to settle the soil in around the roots (water-in). Hold off from starting a fertilizer routine for about three weeks. This gives the plants time to adjust to their new size and home.

Tiny potted gardens will need to have their roots and stems pruned like this two or three times a year. These gardens can thrive indoors year-round with only 2–3 tablespoons of water every few days or they can go outside for the summer. If you place them outside, however, check often to see that they have enough water; drying winds can be fatal to your tiny pals.

Tip Small "trees" and "greenery" add a lot to toy train countrysides and doll house landscaping and gardens, but don't forget that they are *not* plastic and need to be fed, watered, and cared for like full-size plants.

19

Making Baby Plants—the Fine Art of Propagation

What You Need

Seeds

Seedling potting soil

Margarine tubs, egg cartons, sawed-off milk cartons, compressed peat pots, seedling flats (in other words, almost anything goes!)

Ice-cream sticks for garden stakes and black permanent marker

Fertilizer

Small pots (or market packs) and all-purpose potting soil

What You Do

Many people live where the seasons change. Some months it is just too cold to garden outside; that's when you can discover "the great indoors."

Use your winter windowsill as a laboratory to grow more of all kinds of plants and you won't have to spend your birthday cash and earned money at a garden center buying some. There are several ways to get a lot of new plants.

STARTING SEEDS

Most of the plants needed for the projects in this book can be easily grown from seed.

Send away for seed catalogs during the winter. Study them closely when they arrive in the mail. Buy the seeds you want through the mail or from seed racks at your local hardware or garden store (they cost much less than plants). Look on the package for the "packed for" year; you will get better results from fresh, not old, seeds.

Sow seeds according to the directions on the back of the seed packet. Pay special attention to the sowing time. You don't want to start fast-growing plants too early in the season. Make sure to cover the seed with an additional light layer of seedling soil, if it's called for on the package. The instructions will also tell you how long it takes for the seed of that plant to germinate, or start growing. (If the number of days needed for germination has passed and you don't see the seedlings, and it's not because you forgot to provide proper moisture, return the seed package to the supplier for a replacement packet of seeds.)

Remember to label the rows of seed you've sown. Write the names on ice-cream sticks. You can also attach part or all of the seed packet to the stick as information, to inspire you, and to remind you what the plants will look like when they are fully grown.

When seedlings first emerge from the soil they send up two "seed" leaves. These first leaves don't look at all like the true leaves that will follow. If you don't label your seeds when you sow them, you won't know which is which when they come up.

Seedlings should be fertilized at *half* the recommended rate until they are transplanted, when their true leaves appear. The recommended fertilizer rates are found on the back of the package of plant food.

When the seedlings become too cramped in their seed bed, it's time to move them. Fill market packs or small pots with all-purpose potting soil. Gently take a small pinch of seedlings (or use a small spoon if you prefer) and tuck the roots into the center of the pot. Water-in so the soil will settle around the roots. Water and fertilize the growing plants (at the recommended rate), while you wait for the weather to warm up enough to set plants outside.

ROOTING A LEAF

Another way to get new plants is by using a part of the plant itself, called cloning.

What You Need

Margarine tub or other small container

Potting or specialized African violet soil

Leaf from African violet plant. Ask permission to take one from a healthy mature plant. You need a leaf with part of the stem still on it. Use a sharp knife, or break the stem off cleanly. (Buy a plant only as a last resort.)

What You Do

Fill margarine tub ⅔ full with potting soil. Bury the stem and the bottom ⅓ of the leaf in the soil. Place the leaf cutting in a window location that gets bright light, but *not* in direct sunlight, and water evenly.

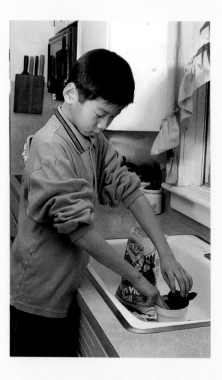

Check the tub a couple of times each week to see if it needs watering. The soil should not be allowed to dry out completely or the delicate new roots will die. In 8 to 10 weeks, the leaf will form a new plantlet that you can move into its own small pot.

ROOTING TIP CUTTINGS

What You Need

Clear glass or jar of water

Sharp knife

Healthy houseplant, such as Swedish Ivy

Small pot with potting soil

Fertilizer

What You Do

Cut a healthy growing tip from the houseplant. A plant with long vines or lots of space between the leaves and stems makes it easier to get the portion of stem you need. The length of the cutting should be about 2½ inches (6.5 cm) long.

Remove the lower leaves; a portion of stem without leaves is more likely to form roots.

Place the cutting, or two or more, in water and wait 4 to 8 weeks. Change the water once each week during the rooting process. As roots start to appear, you can add a little fertilizer to the water. Once a cutting has a good set of roots, it can be transplanted into a container of potting soil.

23

DIVIDE AND CONQUER

What You Need

Overgrown houseplant (many stems going into the soil)

Sharp knife and cutting board

Several pots with potting soil

What You Do

Knock the plant out of its pot by turning it upside down and tapping the rim of the pot against a hard object. Apply steady pressure on the stems (in other words "pull its hair"). Do this over an old tablecloth or newspapers, so you don't have to worry about the soil making a big mess. Most of it will likely be bound up by the old overgrown root ball.

Carefully slice the plant in half, starting at the crown (soil line) and cutting downwards towards the root ball. Gently pull the halves apart.

Divide the halves again, if more plants are desired. Plant the separated sections in their own pots and water-in.

24

Rabbit's-foot Fern

Good Plants for Tip Cutting
Ivy *(Hedera)*
Purple Passion Vine *(Gynura)*
Pothos *(Epipremnum)*
Swedish Ivy *(Plectranthus)*

Good Plants for Leaf Cutting
African Violets *(Saintpaulia)*

Good Plants to Divide
Rabbit's-foot Fern *(Davallia)*
Artillery plant *(Pilea)*
Sentry Palm *(Howea)*

Artillery plant

Ivy

Sentry Palm

Pothos

Purple Passion Vine   African Violets

Swedish Ivy

25

A Fungus Amongus!

Growing your own edible mushrooms is fun and easy with a specially built "hideout tent" for these fungal friends.

What You Need

Inoculated mushroom kit

Garden hand-clipper or sharp knife

Large foil baking pan

Clear dry cleaner's plastic bag

4 tree twigs, about 24 inches (60 cm) long

Hole punch

Large twist tie or twine

What You Do

Write away to a mushroom farm to order a pre-inoculated edible-mushroom kit, a closed bag of sawdust with mushroom spores (their special seed) mixed in. When you write, it might be a good idea to tell them you are a kid just starting out and let them direct you to the easiest types to grow.

When your kit arrives, unpack and examine the contents right away to make sure nothing has been damaged. Too, spores are usually guaranteed for only one month from the date they are shipped, so you can't wait very long to complete this project.

In nature, mushrooms grow in moist, shady forests; so to grow

them you need to provide similar conditions. You can do this by building a humidity tent.

* Take 4 same-length tree twigs, and clip off the side branches to make single clean stalks.
* With a punch, sharp pencil, or nail, make holes in each corner of the baking pan.
* Insert the four twigs into the holes and bend them to meet at the top. Bind them together with a twist tie or strong string.

Place the mushroom kit in the baking pan and put about 1 inch (2.5 cm) of water in the bottom of the pan. The evaporating water will provide the extra humidity the mushrooms need. Place the plastic bag over it and close. Check the humidity in the tent every two or

three days. When the bottom of the pan is dry, add more water by pouring it over the top of the kit.

Mushrooms grow very quickly; they can double in size overnight! Within a week, you should see your new fungal friends growing out of the inner bag.

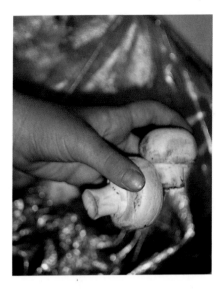

Examine the first few mushrooms that appear. Notice that the mushroom tops are rounded like small umbrellas. This is the time to pick them. If a mushroom gets too old, the head will collapse like a broken umbrella.

To pick the mushrooms, simply twist them at the bottom of the stalk where they pop out of the inner bag. Wash, dry, and slice your harvested mushrooms. They are wonderful raw in salads or sautéed in butter with fresh parsley. Sneak a few onto your next pizza and say, "Hey, there's a fungus amongus!"

The Tough Get Growing

Not everyone has a green thumb. The good news is there are some plants that will grow even if you ignore them. Cacti are tough—no T.L.C. needed here. Give them sun and a dry soil and they'll thrive. But no petting a cactus!

What You Need

Margarine tub, or other shallow, wide container, with holes in the bottom

Sand

Potting soil

Colored gravel (optional)

Tablespoon and tongs

Cactus plants

What You Do

Shop for cacti at your local garden center. For best value, look for overgrown ones that just need larger pots to be happy. (This goes for buying other types of plants, too.)

In a large container, mix sand and potting soil together in equal amounts. Fill your garden container about halfway or a little more with the sandy soil mix.

Carefully remove the cactus plants from their smaller pots; use tongs to avoid the prickly needles. With tablespoon and tongs, plant the cacti in the sandy soil. Keep in mind that cacti are very top-heavy. Once you have your prickly pals in place, use the spoon to backfill

and press the soil tightly against each plant in the container.

If you wish, place colored gravel on top of the soil as a decorative mulch and you will have the coolest desert in the neighborhood.

Caring for a cactus garden is easy. Put it in the sunniest window in the house. Cacti also enjoy being outside over the summer. Watering once a month is fine. You will not need to fertilize at all the first year, and only once or twice each following growing season. (Now that's what I call *tough*!)

Is It Spring Yet?

Sometimes winter seems to last a very long time. You can, however, put a little "spring in your step," and in your nose, by planting and forcing bulbs.

What You Need

Shallow flowerpot

Paper-white narcissus bulbs (or precooled *hyacinths)*

Pebbles or sand and potting soil

What You Do

Purchase Paper-white *(Narcissus tazetta)* bulbs at your local garden center, or hardware or variety store. When buying bulbs, pretend you are shopping for apples. You want to buy the biggest ones in the bin. Look for firm bulbs, with no soft or rotten spots on them. Paper-white bulbs are usually available in stores at the first sign of winter. Other bulbs are

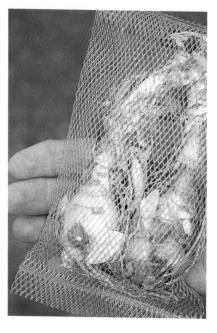

displayed throughout the fall, but unless precooled, they must be planted outdoors to trigger them into spring flowering.

Fill a shallow pot halfway with either pebbles or a combination of potting soil and sand mixed half and half. Place the bulbs in the pot (with the pointy end up), putting one in the middle and then the others in a circle around it. It is O.K. if the bulbs crowd together, touching each another: they grow well in tight quarters.

Sprinkle more pebbles or potting soil/sand mix on top of the bulbs. Don't cover up these bulbs completely, Paper-white bulbs seem to like getting some light and air.

If you end up with an extra bulb, try growing it separately in a tall, clear drinking glass so that you can watch it put out roots. Put a handful of marbles or clean pebbles in the bottom of the glass so the bulb sits partially out of water. Otherwise, the directions are the same.

Place your garden on a windowsill that gets plenty of daylight and is cool at night. One great thing about Paper-whites is that you don't have to provide the cooling period that most other bulbs need before they will flower. In other words, you've done all you need to.

Check your bulb garden now and then for water. The sandy soil or pebbles can dry out between

waterings, but the garden should not go bone-dry for a long period of time.

Another nice thing about Paper-whites (and bulbs in general) is that they don't need to be fertilized during the forcing process. Like a kid who always has a lunch bag with him, a bulb has its own food conveniently packed up inside it. This is why you want to select big bulbs: the bigger the bulb, the more the nourishment and the bigger the flowers.

As the leaves start to push out of the bulbs, you may notice that they grow towards the sun. Make it a point to check on them often and to turn the pot every couple of days. This will make the plants grow up straight.

You can expect to see, and smell, Paper-white flowers within 4 to 6 weeks of the planting date.

Paper-whites have a strong, sweet scent. If the smell is too strong for you, place the pot in a back room and leave the door open just a crack. (As with aerosol room freshener, you might like the

scent but not want to use the whole can at once.) Cut off a few stalks of Paper-white to share with a neighbor or friend—a little goes a long way. They'll enjoy an early touch of spring, too.

When you are finished enjoying the flowers, simply stop watering and discard. Paper-white bulbs are inexpensive to buy and not the kind that send up flowers again year after year.

Tricking Bulbs

Other than Paper-whites, to grow most bulbs indoors you need to trick them. They need to go through a cool (winter) period before they will flower. To try growing these other bulbs, purchase a few in the fall, place them in plastic bags, and store them in the refrigerator for two full months. If you are able to find precooled bulbs from your local garden center or get them from a mail-order bulb company, you can skip this step and still enjoy flowering bulbs all year long.

Fertilizer Hints

On every package of fertilizer you will see three numbers. What these numbers do is tell you, the gardener, how strong the fertilizer is. In most cases, you will want to choose fertilizer in which all the numbers are the same. A 5–5–5 or a 10–10–10 fertilizer, for example, has an equal balance of N–P–K (Nitrogen–Phosphorus–Potassium). With bulbs, look for fertilizer with a larger middle number, such as 5–10–5. This means that the fertilizer supplies more phosphorus, needed for strong roots. Since the root (actually the bulb in this case) means everything in recycling bulbs, a diet rich in phosphorus will help to ensure success with the next year's flowers.

Growing Bigger Bulbs

If you selected and grew precooled hyacinth bulbs instead of Paper-whites, they can be saved to bloom again the following year. Now you need to let the bulbs dry out and die down on their own. This dying process is an important part of growing bulbs. The leaves that stay in the container garden long after the flowers are gone are the plant's food factory. They are hard at work refilling the bulb's "bag lunch" with the food that will be needed for the next season's flowers. Right after your hyacinths have bloomed, add some of the special bulb fertilizer to the potting soil/sand mix or pebbles. This will allow the bulbs to take up any nutrients they may need to make even bigger bulbs.

Tiptoe Through the Tulips

What You Need

Tulip bulbs

Wooden box or other container that drains well

Potting soil and sand

Bulb fertilizer

Grass seed (optional)

3–5 bags of leaves

What You Do

In the fall, rake up some leaves (maybe you can earn money for gardening supplies by doing it). You'll need three to five large bags of leaves to insulate your bulb garden all winter long.

Next, pick up some early spring bulbs, like tulips, at a garden center or chain store's fall display. You'll have a lot to choose from. Besides tulips, there are daffodils

Imagine a clear, bright day in early spring. The sun is shining, birds are singing, bees are visiting every tulip in your fabulous container garden. Sound great? To make it happen, you need to plan ahead. Tulips *(Tulipa)* and other spring-flowering bulbs must be planted in the fall.

the bulbs as little brats, and plant them with their pointy noses stuck up in the air. Then, cover the bulbs completely, so you can't even see the tips of their noses. Bulbs are, in fact, sometimes planted quite deep in a regular garden, so, if your container allows, you can bury them deep. Pat the soil down around them and water-in thoroughly.

and hyacinths. All of these bulbs are easy to grow. Experiment and plant as many as you can.

Read the labels carefully, especially when selecting tulips. These flowers come in many colors, shapes, heights, and even bloom times, so you'll have some decisions to make. To get the best value for your bulb money, look for perennials. Perennial means that, after flowering, the bulbs can come up again another spring, so be sure to save them for the next fall's planting. Also, when buying bulbs, remember the "apple rule": Buy the biggest and the best, the same as you do with apples.

Fill your container halfway with a mixture of sand and potting soil.

Add a bulb fertilizer, or bonemeal, following the instructions on the package. Now you are ready to plant.

If you don't want a mishmash of flowers on your hands, open a bag and plant all that variety before you open others. It is almost impossible to tell which bulb is which, once they get mixed up. Inspect the bulbs as you plant, and discard any that are soft, rotted, or that you are in doubt about.

In order to flower, the bulbs must be planted right side up. The *top* of a bulb is *pointed*. Think of

Set the container aside in a cool spot out of direct sunlight as winter approaches. After the first hard frost, take your bags of leaves and tuck them around and on top of your bulb garden container as insulation. So you won't have to chase rolling leaf bags all winter long, choose a protected place for your bulbs' winter sleep or weight the bags down.

When you see early signs of spring, such as robins and swelling buds on shrubs, remove the bagged leaves. Bulbs don't mind cooler temperatures, so this can be done weeks before your local frost-free date. Water the bulb garden as needed, and enjoy your spring garden.

Tip Sprinkle grass seed on top of the container soil and, as temperatures warm, lush green grass will complement the lovely flowering bulbs.

Bulb Care and Storage

Like all bulbs, tulips need a rest after flowering. The great thing about container gardening is that you can put unsightly gardens out of sight while the plants take nourishment from the soil and build up their bulbs again for the next flowering season.

After the growth has died down on its own, dig the bulbs up, shake off the excess soil, and store them dry in small paper bags labelled with the color and variety of the bulbs. Place them in a cool place (like a basement) over the summer. Before long, you will be tiptoeing down the basement stairs to replant them next fall!

Gardens on Parade

What can you do with those old, worn-out shoes you keep outgrowing? Stuff those smelly sneakers with plants—they won't care. It doesn't even matter if you lost a shoe, and only have one left. In fact, one's just right!

What You Need

Old shoes or boots

Potting soil

Fertilizer

Plants or seeds

What You Do

Poke several holes in the upper part of the shoe *just above the sole* for drainage (the sole itself is often too tough). Fill the shoes with potting soil.

You can plant shoes either with seeds of a quick-growing plant, such as basil or zinnia, some rooted cuttings, or extra transplants from other projects.

Give some thought to the containers. High-top sneakers give the best stability, so they would be your best choice for taller flowering plants. Short material can go into loafers, the toes of high heels, baby shoes, even slippers. (Stay away from sandals; the soil slips through the straps!)

Walk your gardens outside, after your local frost-free date, to an area that gets the correct amount of sun for the type of plant used. You might place a couple of shoe gardens on the front stoop for passersby to enjoy and shake their heads at.

Herbs for the Furry Set

Show your love for your pet by making a special collar that looks good, smells good, and repels insects—all at the same time!

What You Need

Large flowerpot

Potting soil

Herbs, including insect-repelling tansy lavender and pennyroyal mint, and deodorizing pineapple sage, rosemary, and lemon balm

Garden clippers

Handkerchief (small pets) or bandanna (large pets)

Safety pin

Tip For feline friends, why not grow some catnip as a special treat? Cats and kittens become especially playful when this herb is around. (Their games and joyful antics will keep you chuckling, and remember, laughter is contagious!)

Catnip, or *Nepeta cataria*, can be easily grown from seed or cuttings. A perennial, it can stay outside during cold weather or grow indoors. Harvest the leaves of outdoor plants before frost. Dry them, roll them in scraps of cloth, and tie the ends, and you have fresh catnip toys purr-fect for holiday giving.

What You Do

Most of these herbs are either hard to find in seed form or are very slow growing from seed. If you don't know a neighbor or friend who has these herbs, take a trip to your local garden center and buy the smallest pots of herbs available. If you ask—especially if you are a regular customer—some places may let you clip a few cuttings to root your own plants. Once the cuttings have rooted, the plants grow fast. Repot the rooted cuttings and you will have an herb garden good for your pet and your pocketbook.

Place the container herb garden in a sunny place. Remember that herbs like it hot and on the dry side. Don't fertilize more than once a month. By keeping the plants "hungry," the herbs' oils will be stronger and do a better job "freshening" your pet's scent and repelling insects.

When the plants grow full in the pot, you can start harvesting the leaves. Trim off an assortment of the herbs to create a perfect blend for your pet's collar. Roll the cut herbs vigorously between the palms of your hands to release some of the oils.

Spread the handkerchief or bandanna flat and place your herbal recipe in a line reaching towards opposite corners (diagonally). Fold the square cloth once to form a triangle. Then tuck the herbs in from the end corners and roll the bandanna tightly into an herb "sausage" and pin.

Twist the ends and tie the herbal collar around your pet's neck. Change it every week. Wash out the bandanna or handkerchief before refilling with more herbs.

Personality Pots

appear. A pair of luscious lips is a nice touch. Long, dangling legs with small stones as feet will keep another "radical" radish on his toes.

If there's still room on your windowsill, a green-haired friend or two, and then some amazing sprouting potatoes, will liven things up.

What You Need

Styrofoam cup

Colored markers or crayons

Stick-on eyes

Felt or construction paper

Glue

Radish seeds

Potting soil

Gravel or pebbles

What You Do

Perhaps creating the face and figure for your "radish top" is at the top of your to-do list. If so, create away! It is also fine to decorate the pots after sprouts

Then, place a layer of gravel or pebbles in the cup for drainage. Fill the cup to the rim with moistened potting soil. Sow the radish seeds according to directions. Cover the seeds lightly and gently pat the soil down. Place the cup on a sunny windowsill and wait a week to ten days for green "hair" to appear.

Make sure to keep the soil evenly watered as the seedlings emerge. Notice that the plants have a tendency to grow towards the light. Be sure to rotate the cup daily so the stems will grow straight.

Potato Pals

What You Need

Sweet potato

Baking potato

Strong toothpicks

Water

2 clear, large-mouthed jars

Assorted odds and ends, for dress-up

What You Do

Select a sweet potato and a baking potato from the grocery store. Fill up two large-mouthed jars halfway with water. Stick three heavy-duty toothpicks into each potato and sit them in a sunny window for six to eight weeks.

Finally, let the creative juices flow. Collect odds and ends to adorn your new pals. The thing about potato people is, it's so easy to grow to like them!

No more room on your windowsill? If sunlight isn't available, set up a garden under artificial light.

Position several houseplants together on a plastic tray (metal will rust) under a fluorescent light. Raise the tray, or lower the light, so that the plants and light are no closer than 6 inches (15 cm) and no farther than 24 inches (60 cm) apart. You might place some pebbles in the tray and make a reservoir for extra water to evaporate. Some plants enjoy the extra humidity that this setup provides.

The lights don't need to be on all the time. (Plants enjoy a rest time, too.) To remind you to turn the light off and on, paste a paper-flower cutout on your bathroom mirror where you'll see it when you brush your teeth (morning and night). If you should forget to turn the light off now and then, it won't hurt the plants. Also, fluorescent lights don't heat up or use much energy. If you use an automatic timer instead, set it to turn the lights on for 12 to 14 hours each day.

Summer Party Centerpiece

Here is a cool idea for a special container garden to brighten up any summer party.

What You Need

½ large watermelon (cut lengthwise)

Large spoon

Bowl

Potting soil

Summer-blooming annual plants

What You Do

With a spoon, scoop out the pink watermelon and place it in a bowl where hungry friends and everyone can dig in.

Fill the watermelon rind with potting soil. Plant a mixture of colorful summer annuals and

water thoroughly. (This is a short-term project. You will want to throw out the container after two or three days.)

Tip Why not save some of the mature watermelon seeds? Wipe them off and let them dry for a day or two in the sun. Put them in a clean envelope and store them in a dry place. Next spring, when the soil warms up, plant them outside in the ground. With a little luck, you might be able to enjoy the fruits of your own watermelon patch next year.

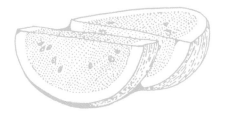

Strawflowers—from Seed to Craft

If you like using flowers to decorate craftwork, you'll love having bunches of colorful, home-grown strawflowers *(Helichrysum)* to choose from.

What You Need

First

Strawflower seeds

Seedling potting soil (small package)

Small margarine container

Spray bottle of water

Next

Teaspoon

2 foam egg cartons or small plastic pots

Regular potting soil

Then

Window box

Regular potting soil

Trowel or large spoon

What You Do

First

In early spring, fill container with *seedling* potting soil (has fertilizer in it, just right for starting baby plants). Sprinkle seeds according to directions on the package. Water with a spray bottle and check daily to make sure the soil does not dry out. It should feel moist to the

touch but not soaking wet.

Keep the container indoors, in a sunny window with no drafts. Daytime room temperature should be between 65 and 70°F (19–21°C)—a place where you feel comfortable and wouldn't have to wear a sweater. Baby plants like the same temperatures that you do.

Next (about three weeks later)

When you see a second set of

leaves on the baby plants, it is time to transplant. Fill egg cartons or plastic pots with regular potting soil. Use a small spoon to gently dig the seedlings out of the margarine container. Place two or three baby plants in each section of the egg carton or separate pot. Water-in gently, still using the spray bottle of water.

After a week or two, add some fertilizer to the water. Have an adult help you follow the directions on the fertilizer package. Because you are dealing with small plants, mix the fertilizer to half the

recommended rate. These babies are not ready for adult-strength fertilizer. Just as there are adults' and children's medicines, fertilizers for plants must be taken in doses that are safe for baby and adult plants.

Check the plants and water every two or three days. Keep an eye on the weather as the plants grow.

Then

When the danger of frost in your area has passed, you may put the growing plants outside. Fill a

window box with potting soil. Pop the strawflower plants out of the egg cartons or small pots and place them in a window box. You can now give them adult-strength fertilizer once every three to four weeks. Water regularly and evenly as needed.

By summer's end or early fall, your window box will be full of colorful strawflower blossoms. Now is the time to harvest. Strawflowers are special because they look nice both on and off the plant. With cut flowers, the cutting and drying process is tricky. Strawflowers are easy and fun to work with because, actually, the blooms themselves are already dried!

To harvest, simply cut the flower stems right at the soil line. This gives the cut flowers really long stems, making them easier to tie strings to for drying the foliage. Freshly cut bunches of strawflowers must be hung upside down until the stems and leaves are dry. By hanging them flower-down, gravity keeps the stems straight, and bunches of dried flowers can be made into arrangements for year-round decoration.

Strawflower heads are easily removed from the stems for use in craft work, such as being glued to a backing for a beautiful picture frame. However you use the flowers, the colors will not fade and you will always be reminded of the time you grew your own strawflowers.

Pumpkin Pots for Everyone

Pumpkins are great fun, but not just for scary Halloween faces.

Try this version of Peter Peter Pumpkin Eater's idea. Plant pansies in a pumpkin shell and you can keep them very well.

What You Need

Medium-size pumpkin

Sharp knife

Large spoon for scooping

Fall-blooming pansies (Viola)

Potting soil

What You Do

Cut open the top of the pumpkin and scoop out the "guts" as you would for making a jack-o'-lantern. Turn the pumpkin shell over and cut three tiny triangles out of the bottom for drainage.

Fill the pumpkin shell with potting soil. Plant 3 or 4 fall-blooming pansies in the pumpkin. If you plan early, you can start your own pansies from seed in the middle of summer or buy them from your local garden center when you are out selecting a pumpkin you like. Water your pumpkin garden as needed. Since this is a short-term project (pumpkins don't last forever), there is no need to fertilize.

At the first heavy frost, pick up your pumpkin pot and toss it into the garbage or a compost pile. Hard frost will make the pumpkin soft and mushy, and you won't want to handle it then.

While tossing the pumpkin pot is sound advice, you could save the pansies. They will survive the winter if transplanted to a large container outside with fresh potting soil and protection from drying winter winds. During the winter months, the leaves will look as if they are suffering, but as spring arrives and the soil in the container warms up, you will see new growth emerge. Your pumpkin pansies will bloom again, all spring long!

That Monster Tomato Needs a Cage!

What You Need

Bushel basket, or other large tub

Large garbage bag

Potting soil

Watering can or hose with sprinkler head

Plant fertilizer

Large-fruit tomato plant

Tomato cage, from garden center

Growing regular-size tomatoes in containers is fun and easy. When growing large-fruit varieties (monsters), there are special things to consider. Caging your monster tomato plant will help you keep things under control.

What You Do

After the danger of frost has passed, start off by lining your bushel basket with the large garbage-can bag. (Some containers may not need lining, but a bushel basket will leak if you don't.) Lined baskets can last for several growing seasons, to be used over and over again. Fill your lined basket with potting soil. (Tomatoes like

moist—not wet—soil, so don't add drainage for this project.)

Dig a hole in the middle of the basket and plant your tomato plant. Keep the tag that comes with the plant and stick it into the soil. This will help you remember next year what variety you grew. (You can also grow your own starter plants from seeds.) Take care not to set the plant too deep or shallow in the basket. The soil line in the basket should be the same as it was in the transplant pot.

Place the cage over the plant. It is easier to cage a small monster than a large one. The cage will support the plant as it grows taller. Tomatoes are heavy fruit. In a regular garden, tomatoes that are growing often rest on the ground if stems are not staked, which is not

good. By using a cage, the growth will have good support and the fruit will get plenty of sunlight, which will give you nicer tomatoes.

So the basket will look neat, trim or fold in the edges of the liner bag. Water-in your tomato right after you transplant. Be sure the soil settles down around the roots. Move the basket to where it will get full sun. Water and fertilize the plant as it grows. If you notice some yellowing leaves, it's a sign that the plant needs food. To avoid this, you will probably have to add fertilizer to your water every other week. (Remember, you're feeding a monster; they like to eat a lot.)

It's an exciting time when your plant starts to make small yellow flowers. These flowers are what will eventually turn into the delicious monster tomatoes. When the plant gets heavy with ripening fruit, it is time to harvest it. This will happen in mid- to late summer.

You can remove the fruit when it is either fully or partially red. Unless you like fried green tomatoes, do not pick the fruit when it is all green or it will never ripen. Tomatoes picked half-ripe can be placed on a sunny windowsill and, in two or three days, they will be ready to eat.

Be sure to harvest all the fruit on the vine that is ripe. If you don't pick ripe tomatoes, they will begin to rot, and rotting fruit attracts bugs that love to nibble at monsters. If you stay on top of

your picking, you can expect monster tomatoes from late summer until frost.

After your first hard frost, throw out your tomato plant, but save the cage and basket to use again next year.

Tip Even if you have to buy a four-pack of tomatoes, plant only one in the basket. Plant the others elsewhere or give them to friends. It's better to grow just one tomato plant with a lot of love and attention than to crowd four into the same pot and get poor performance.

Salad on a Stick

A planting stick is nice to have, if you have an adult to help you make one. If not, a special basket (or separate containers) will do to celebrate that green-headed salad star, the great and wonderful lettuce!

What You Need

Potting soil

Lettuce plants

Fertilizer

Planting stick (see instructions) or Belden basket

What You Do

With your planting stick or Belden basket ready and waiting, select the type of lettuce you want to grow. There are many varieties to choose from, so study the seed packets in stores in early spring.

To grow seeds, start them indoors early in a warm, sunny window. In about four weeks, you can transplant the baby lettuce heads into market packs or separate small pots. After the plants are established, which should take about two weeks, they will be ready for the next step.

Once the danger of frost has passed, fill the four pockets of the stick or all openings of a Belden basket with moistened potting soil. Carefully, plug the young plants into position and then water-in. Hang your "salad maker" outdoors in a sunny place that is protected from the wind.

The key to success with this

Red Sail

Buttercrunch

Two-Star

Making a Planting Stick

Take 3 feet (90 cm) of 4-inch (10 cm) diameter PVC pipe. Drill a small hole clear through the pipe about 1½ inches (4 cm) from one end. Feed a wire through the hole and twist it into a loop to hang.

Next, make four markings along the length of the tube. These will be the openings from which the plants will grow. Each opening should be placed one quarter turn around the stick so that the planting stick will balance while the plants grow. Cut out the openings with a hacksaw.

Using a larger, ⁵⁄₁₆-inch (8 mm) bit, drill two holes 3 inches (7.5 cm) below each opening, going through to the opposite side. Cut eight 5-inch (13 cm) dowels and insert them, or pencils, into each set of drilled holes— all four levels.

Lay some cotton cloth scraps across the dowels inside the pipe openings. The cloth will trap the soil and moisture needed by the roots of the lettuce heads.

project is the watering. Unhook your Salad on a Stick planter twice a week and feel the soil pockets. To water and fertilize the plants, tilt the stick or basket so that each opening gets the love and attention it needs.

Once the heads of lettuce start to fill in, harvest the outer leaves for salads. As long as the heads are kept happy they will produce long into the season.

Rinse the lettuce leaves thoroughly. Mix in some tasty and colorful vegetables (sliced peppers, carrots, and tomatoes are great) for a tossed salad, and you and your Salad on a Stick will be a big hit.

Petunia Pig

You know how to make friends, but here is a special one that you assemble! All you need are petunias *(Petunia)* and a few items you can find around the house.

What You Need

Round 2-litre plastic bottle with cap

Adult with serrated knife

Nails and a hammer

Pink felt and scissors

Black marker

Strong glue

Potting soil

4 petunia plants in market pack

Long pipe cleaner

4 large corks

What You Do

Ask an adult to cut an opening, large enough to hold four plants, on one side of a clean, dry bottle. (Using a black marker, draw a pattern for the size opening you need beforehand so that it is the right size.) Then have your helper punch four drainage holes in the

the felt strip so that it sticks out about an inch (2.5 cm). Wrap the felt tightly around the pipe cleaner and glue the long edge of the felt. Take a pencil and wrap the tail around it to form a curl. Stick the exposed end of the pipe cleaner through the "tail" hole and wrap it around itself (knot) to attach. Fill

side opposite the bottle's opening, using a large nail and hammer.

Using the hammer and nails again, punch a small hole in the back of the pig so the tail can be attached.

Cut a piece of pink felt about 4 inches (10 cm) square. Cut it again diagonally to make two triangles and glue the edges of each shut, forming the ears. Glue the ears to the bottle, which must be clean and dry, and let the glue dry undisturbed for ten minutes.

Cut another piece of pink felt about 2 by 6 inches (5 x 16 cm). Place a long pipe cleaner inside

your pig container with potting soil, packing it up into Petunia's head first before you fill up her back.

Place four corks underneath to act as Petunia's legs. Practise positioning the corks before you actually glue them on, to be sure that Petunia will stand steady on her feet.

Petunia's petunias can be any color you like. Plant and water them in and place her in a sunny location. Remember to check the soil every three or four days and, if it seems dry, give her a drink. Remove old faded flower buds to keep her looking nice.

If Petunia Pig's leaves should start to yellow, move her out of the constant hot sun and let her "wallow" in the sun for only a few hours a day. Remember, too, that she will need some food, so give her some fertilizer. If the plants should get too tall, it is O.K. to give Petunia a little trim. Pinch the longer stems back to a few inches, and in a couple of weeks she'll look better than ever.

Triple-Treat Garden

Pen and pencil

Scissors

Pin and nail

Measuring stick

Masking tape

Black marker

Small pots of edible flowers:
    2 *Johnny-jump-ups* (Viola)
    4 *Calendulas* (Calendula)
    6 *Nasturtiums* (Tropaeolum)

You can make a container garden that not only stacks up 1 - 2 - 3, but is pretty and edible as well.

What You Need

3 aluminum baking dishes: 1 small, 1 medium, 1 large

Twine

Hole punch

Plastic margarine-tub lid

What You Do

Punch holes in the four corners of each baking dish. Draw 12 small circles on the lid with a pen and using a dime as the pattern. Cut out the circles and pierce the center of each with a pin. Using a nail, make the hole bigger until twine will fit through it.

    Measure out and cut four 5-foot (153 cm) lengths of twine. Tie the four pieces of twine together at one end and make a loop for hanging.

Tape the other loose ends to prevent unravelling.

Lay the twine flat and, from the loop end, mark off each piece of twine at 18-inch (46 cm) intervals. Do this three times. Each string should have 3 markings on it, spaced 18 inches (46 cm) apart.

With the loop side up, thread the smallest baking dish onto the twine through the punched holes. Slide one of the small plastic discs onto each piece of twine, up to the highest marks. Carefully knot each twine at the marking, making sure that the plastic disc is *above* the knot.

Repeat this entire process with the medium-size and then the large-size baking dish. Trim off any excess twine and place the plants in pans as follows: Johnny-jump-ups on top, calendulas in the middle, and nasturtiums in the bottom baking dish. Water and fertilize as you would any other garden.

Your Bottom-Up Treats

* Pick nasturtium flowers and leaves and sprinkle them into a salad.

* Calendula flower petals planted in a soup bowl really perk up canned tomato soup. Edible decorations are great!

* Pick off Johnny-jump-up flowers and float them in a glass of ginger ale for a delicious and pretty drink. Enjoy a "Johnny and Ginger" by eating the Johnnies while you sip.

Time for a Sundial Garden

Did you ever lose track of the time while gardening? Solve that problem by making your own clock garden, using sun and shadows!

What You Need

Old car tire

Small can of white exterior latex paint

Wide paintbrush

Long straight stick or dowel

Black permanent marker

Cloth, about 3 feet (90 cm) square

Measuring stick

Potting soil

Short, sun-loving flowers (about 5) in small pots

Watch or clock

What You Do

Find an old tire and roll it over to a sunny spot. Wipe the tire dry and clean of loose dirt. Paint it white and let it dry overnight.

With the black marker, make dark lines dividing the tire into four equal sections. (Think of the tire as a large pie being cut into

four equal slices.) Near each marked line, write a number (12, 3, 6, and 9) in its appropriate place, as it appears on a clockface or watch. Copying the watch exactly, write the other numbers in position. Go over the numbers several times with the black marker so that they really show up against the white tire.

Spread a cloth out in the middle of the tire and fill it with potting soil. Trim or tuck in extra cloth so that the clockface is clearly visible.

It is important to choose flowers that love a lot of sunshine, since this garden must get the full sun in order to work. Too, select plants that will not grow very tall. Choose those that grow only 10 inches (25 cm) or less. If taller plants are used, their shadows will shade the numbers on the tire, and your sundial will not work. Water and fertilize your sundial garden like any container garden.

To set the time, pick a sunny day. Place a long stick right in the center of the tire flower garden. At exactly twelve noon, shift the tire around so that the shadow of the stick falls exactly on the marker line labelled 12. Now that your sundial clock is set, be careful not to turn the tire around anymore or move the stick in the center. The straightness of the stick and the positioning of the numbers on the tire are what makes the sundial accurate. Now you'll have no excuse to be late for supper— unless it's cloudy!

Grow an Herb Pillow

Can't find any containers around the house? Not to worry; plunge herb plants right into a bag of potting soil. An herb pillow is a handy garden to have around, especially near the kitchen.

What You Need

Medium-size bag of potting soil

Black marker

Scissors

5 cooking-herb plants in small pots; select from:
    Basil (Ocimum)
    Chive (Allium)
    Dill (Anethum)
    Fennel (Foeniculum)
    French tarragon (Artemisia)
    Mint (Mentha)
    Parsley (Petroselinum)
    Sage (Salvia)

Fertilizer

What You Do

On a flattened bag of potting soil, use a marker to make five X's. Place three of the X's in the back row and two in the front. Working with one X at a time, cut a hole with scissors. Gently move the soil aside or, if space is tight, dig some soil out of the bag to allow space for the root ball. Plant one of the herb plants in the pillow. Do the same for each remaining herb.

Place the finished herb pillow in a sunny location near your kitchen door. The closer the herbs are to the kitchen, the more likely they will actually be used in cooking. Water-in each plant through its own opening in the soil bag.

To keep things neat, the herb pillow can't have drainage holes, so you must drip some water into the planting holes only when the herbs are just about to wilt. Add fertilizer only once a month.

Let the Fun Begin

When you are ready to be a chef, your herb pillow will be ready for you.

It is best to pick herbs the same day you plan to use them. Always wash and dry them before using them in cooking. They can also be stored in the refrigerator for a few hours if necessary.

Harvested herbs may need about two weeks to regrow. When the plants put out new leaves, you can pick some again.

garlic (optional), ½ cup of Parmesan cheese, salt and pepper. Pour mixture over cooked pasta and stir well. Cool in the refrigerator.

* Take a tiny pinch of chopped fennel leaves or seeds and dress the tops of uncooked sugar cookies. Bake according to cookie recipe directions. A lovely licorice flavor will bake in.

Here are some ideas for using your home-grown herbs:
* Mix up iced tea and some fresh lemon. Add a sprig of mint.
* Steam a bag of baby carrots. Drain off water and add 1 tablespoon of butter, 2 tablespoons of honey, and 1 teaspoon of finely chopped dill leaves.
* Mix 2 to 3 tablespoons of finely chopped chives in a pint of sour cream. Drizzle onto a hot baked potato.
* Combine (in a blender or food processor) 1 cup of basil leaves, ½ cup of olive oil, 1 small clove of

Happy Holidays Winter Garden

What You Need

Small evergreen (Dwarf Alberta Spruce shown)

Shovel or trowel

Garden fork

Large outdoor container filled with potting soil

Strong adult, to help plant tree and position container

Popcorn, pinecones, winter berries, peanut butter, birdseed, fruit

Just because it is cold outside is no reason you can't have a container garden. Friends and family can enjoy a holiday garden and birds can eat from it all winter long while they wait for spring.

What You Do

After the first hard frost, use a garden fork to dig old annuals out of large containers. You may need to add more potting soil to replace old soil trapped in the root balls of discarded plants. Mix it in well.

Buy or dig up a small evergreen tree for planting. The Dwarf Alberta Spruce is recommended

Tip For an added spring surprise after a chilly winter, bury some bulbs around the base of the tree to bloom as warmer weather arrives.

because it grows very slowly and can remain in a large outdoor planter for several years. These evergreens are readily available at reasonable prices in chain stores just before the holidays.

If you have permission to dig up a small tree on someone's property, ask an adult to help you and to move it into place in the hole in the center of the container.

Backfill the hole with the potting soil moved aside. Be sure to pack the soil down firmly around the roots with your hands. Water thoroughly.

After a few weeks have passed and your little tree has settled in, start thinking about decorations. Popcorn and winter berries like holly are not only pretty but offer the wintering birds something to

eat. Make more tasty snacks for your feathered friends by filling pinecones with peanut butter and rolling them in birdseed. Hang them on the tree with yarn or pipe cleaners and add a few fruit slices for dessert. A feast for the birds and fun for everyone!

Plants to Know and Grow

Plants have two names: a common name and a scientific name. Sometimes these names are the same. The scientific name is the one officially used by gardeners all over the world. Try to learn the scientific names of plants (given in parenthesis); someday you may want to write to a pen pal in another country about plants and gardening.

Light requirements, height of mature plants and additional information are also provided here.

Browallia *(Browallia)*

Partial shade, 10–18 inches (25–46 cm). Flower colors: blue, purple, or white. Foliage: green. Care: Fertilize often, but in diluted strengths. Can be grown indoors or out. Propagation: seed or cutting.

Calendula *(Calendula)*

Full sun or partial shade, 10–12 inches (25–30 cm). Flower colors: orange or yellow. Foliage: green. Care: Performs best in cool temperatures of spring and fall. Flowering will stop in summer when night temperatures reach 80 degrees F

Browallia

(27 C). Average fertilizer and watering requirements. Deadheading will prolong flowering.

Coleus *(Coleus)*

Full sun or partial shade, 6–24 inches (15–60 cm).
Flower color: light blue flower stems usually removed at bud stage. Foliage: Many colors mixed on different-shaped leaves. Care: Pinch out budding flower stem in favor of foliage. Cut plants back to half the length of stem to encourage

Calendula

Coleus

strong bottom branching. Propagation: seed or stem cutting.

Cosmos *(Cosmos bipinnatus)*

Full sun, 18–48 inches (46–122 cm). Flower color: white, pink, or purple-red. Foliage: green. Care: Water and fertilize lightly. Keep plant in area protected from wind. If the plant needs support, put a long garden stake in the middle of the pot and tie the lower leaves and stems to it to hold the plant erect. Propagation: seed.

Dusty Miller *(Senecio)*

Full sun or partial shade, 8–16 inches (20–40 cm).
Flower color: yellow. Foliage: silvery gray. Care: Do not fertilize these plants and water them rarely. Remove flower buds; this plant is prized for its foliage. Pinch back stems when they get too long or floppy. Propagation: seed.

Cosmos

Dusty Miller

Geranium *(Pelargonium)*

Full sun, 12–24 inches (30–60 cm). Flower colors: red, orange, pink, white, or salmon. Foliage: green. Care: Water and feed a lot. Remove old dried-up flowers and yellowed leaves by snapping them off near the base of their stem. This will encourage new blooms throughout the season. Propagation: seed or cutting.

Geranium

Heliotrope

Heliotrope *(Heliotropium)*

Full sun or partial shade, 15–24 inches (38–60 cm).
Flower color: purple and fragrant!
Foliage: dark green. Care: Fertilize every other watering, allowing soil to dry out between waterings. Can winter indoors as a flowering houseplant if cool night (60 degree F–16 C) temperature can be maintained. Propagation: seed or stem cuttings.

Impatiens *(Impatiens)*

Full sun or partial shade, 6–18 inches (15–46 cm).
Flower colors: red, orange, white, pink,

lavender, or purple. Foliage: green or bronze. Care: Likes partial to deep shade, but can tolerate full sun if given extra water. Average water and fertilizer needs. When plants get too floppy, cut stems back to half the height of the plant. In two to three weeks, a new flush of flowers will emerge. Propagation: seed or stem cutting.

Impatiens

Johnny-jump-up *(Viola)*

Full sun or partial shade, 4–8 inches (10–20 cm).
Flower colors: purple, yellow, and white. Foliage: green. Care: Fertilize once a month. Water evenly so soil never completely dries out. Enjoys cool temperatures. Deadheading will prolong flowering and pruning will keep the foliage tight and neat.

Johnny-jump-up

Lobelia *(Lobelia)*

Full sun or partial shade, 4–8 inches (10–20 cm).
Flower colors: blue, purple, or white. Foliage: green or bronze. Care: As heat builds up in late summer, provide extra shade. Trim back slightly after first flush of bloom and provide an extra shot of fertilizer. Although not the best midsummer performer, plants reflower heavily in the fall. Keep soil evenly moist; in other words, don't let it dry out. Propagation: seed.

Lobelia

Marigold (Tagetes patula)

Full sun, 4–12 inches (10–20 cm).
Flower colors: yellow, orange, red, or a
combination. Foliage: green, Care:
Average water and fertilizer needs.
Overfertilizing will cause too much leaf
growth and lessen flowering. Remove old
flowers to keep plants looking great.
Good in combination-planter pots,
because their strong fragrance keeps
insects away. Propagation: seed.

Marigold

Morning Glory

Morning Glory (Ipomea)

Full sun, 5–10 feet (1.5–3 m).
Flower colors: blue, pink, or white.
Foliage: green and bold! Care: Provide
something for the vines to twist on.
Average water and fertilizer needs.
Propagation: seed.

Nasturtium (Tropaeolum)

Full sun, 8–12 inches (20–30 cm).
Flower colors: yellow, red, or orange.
Foliage: green. Care: Do not fertilize at
all, but pay special attention to watering.
As they enjoy full sun, their need for

water is great, but too much water at
one time can cause them to rot. Pinch
back long, leggy stems to keep the plants
looking nice. Propagation: seed.

Nasturtium

Nicotiana (Nicotiana)

Full sun or partial shade, 12–24 inches
(30–60 cm).
Flower colors: white, pink, or magenta.
Foliage: light green. Care: Average
fertilizer and watering needs, but try not
to let soil dry out completely at any
time. These plants will self-sow their
seeds for next year in your pots. Keep an
eye out for babies to replant elsewhere
the next year. Propagation: seed.

Nicotiana

Pansy

Paper-white

Petunia *(Petunia)*

Full sun, 10–18 inches (25–46 cm).
Flower colors: purple, lavender, blue, red,
pink, salmon, or white. Foliage: green.
Care: Fertilize every other time you
water. Let pot dry out between waterings.
Remove dead flowers every day and trim
long, leggy stems whenever needed.
Propagation: seed.

Petunia

Pansy *(Viola)*

Full sun or partial shade, 4–10 inches
(10–25 cm).
Flower colors: orange, purple, blue,
yellow, pink, white, or red. Foliage:
green. Care: Average watering and
fertilizer needs. Look for heat-resistant
varieties; otherwise they perform best in
early spring and fall plantings. Remove
old flowers to encourage more blooms.
Propagation: seed.

Paper-white *(Narcissus)*

Partial shade, 10–14 inches (25–35 cm).
Flower color: white. Foliage: green. Care:
Grow indoors in a cool room where

temperatures do not rise above 60
degrees F (16 C). This will encourage
strong stem growth. No fertilizer is
needed. Keep bulbs well watered all
through forcing process.

Pinks *(Dianthus)*

Full sun or partial shade 4–15 inches
(10–38 cm).
Flower colors: white, salmon, pink, red,
or lavender. Foliage: green to blue-gray.
Care: Since they enjoy sweet soil,

sprinkle a teaspoon of limestone onto the potting soil. Needs average water and fertilizer. May need to replace in midsummer since they don't like the heat. Propagation: seed.

Pinks

Plumed Celosia *(Celosia)*

Full sun, 6–18 inches (15–46 cm). Flower colors: purple, pink, red, apricot, orange, or yellow. Foliage: green. Care: Not too fussy. Likes to be fertilized, but will perform just fine if you forget to feed. Allow soil to dry out completely between waterings. When purchasing in market packs, select "green" plants

Plumed Celosia

(those not yet in flower). Makes a great cut flower. Celosia needs a lot of light, so grow it only outdoors. Propagation: seed or stem cutting.

Portulaca *(Portulaca)*

Full sun, 4–8 inches (10–20 cm). Flower colors: purple, salmon, pink, red, yellow, or white. Foliage: green. Care: Water and fertilize infrequently. These plants like to be hot and dry. (They wish they were cacti!) Propagation: seed.

Portulaca

Sage *(Salvia)*

Scarlet Sage

Full sun or partial shade, 6–18 inches (15–46 cm).
Flower colors: red, coral, purple, or white. Foliage: green.

Blue Sage

Full sun, 6–36 inches (15–92 cm). Flower colors: blue or white. Foliage: green.
Care: Both scarlet and blue sages have average water and fertilizer needs. Pinch off dead flowers to encourage blooms from branches below. Propagation: seed.

Blue Sage

Snapdragon

Scarlet Sage

Snapdragon *(Antirrhinum)*

Full sun, 6–36 inches (15–92 cm).
Flower colors: pink, burgundy, rust,
yellow, red, or white
Foliage: green. Care: Fertilize once a
month, and water only when the soil
dries out. A teaspoon of limestone
sprinkled onto the soil will bring up
acidity level for better growth. Place
these plants in a warm place; they love
the heat. Pinch out the growing tips of
every *second* plant you stick into your
container. This will stagger the bloom
time for a better show in the pot.
Propagation: seed.

Spider Flower *(Cleome)*

Full sun, 3–6 feet (1–2 m).
Flower color: pink, white, or violet.
Foliage: green. Care: Average feeder, but
water heavily on a regular basis. Tip:
This plant will self-sow its seed. Keep
watch in old pots for new seedlings to
pop up the next growing season. They
can easily be moved as babies, so
transplant them then to another garden
somewhere. Propagation: seed.

Spider Flower

Strawflower *(Helichrysum)*

Full sun, 18–30 inches (46–76 cm).
Flower colors: white, red, yellow, pink,
purple, and orange. Foliage: green. Care:
Sprinkle a teaspoon of limestone in the
container, since they like sweet soil. They
also enjoy the heat, so place plant in a
hot area on your patio. Water and
fertilize lightly. Plants may need staking.
Propagation: seed.

Sunflower *(Helianthus)*

Full sun, 2–8 feet (0.5–2.5 m).
Flower colors: yellow (some with black

Strawflower

Sunflower

eyes, some with yellow). Foliage: big and
bold green! Care: Needs average fertilizer
and water; but let soil dry out between
waterings. Tall varieties will need staking
for support. Growing giants require the
largest containers you can find, and
heavy enough not to tip over.
Propagation: seed.

Sweet Allysum *(Lobularia)*

Full sun or partial shade, 4–6 inches
(10–15 cm).
Flower colors: white, pink, or lavender.
Foliage: green. Care: Average water and
fertilizer needs, but can withstand poor
soil. Trim back foliage slightly after first
flush of bloom to encourage more.
Propagation: seed. (Sow seed directly into
final container to skip the whole
transplant process.)

Sweet Allysum

Vinca

Wax Begonia

Zinnia

Vinca *(Catharanthus)*

Full sun or partial shade, 4–18 inches (10–46 cm).
Flower colors: pink or white. Foliage: green. Care: Keep soil evenly moist; it must not dry out. Fertilize once a month. Propagation: seed.

Wax Begonia *(Begonia)*

Full sun or partial shade, 6–12 inches (15–30 cm).
Flower colors: red, pink, or white. Foliage colors: green, variegated green and white, bronze. Care: Give plenty of fertilizer. Allow soil to dry out completely between waterings. Can be grown indoors or out. Propagation: seed or cutting

Zinnia *(Zinnia)*

Full sun, 6–36 inches (15–90 cm).
Flower colors.: white, pink, lavender, red, orange, or yellow. Foliage: green. Care: Average fertilizer and water needs. This plant's foliage is often troubled by disease. To avoid this, water the plant at soil level; do not get any water on the leaves. Good air movement is also very important to keep the leaves looking nice; place your pot in a windy location. Propagation: seed.

Notes About Supplies

Soil

When growing plants, your best chance for success is using good-quality soil. Ready-made potting soil is strongly recommended because:

You know what you are getting. The "soil" you find on an abandoned city lot probably does not possess all the qualities and nutrients needed to grow plants.

It's readily available. Whether you live in a city, in a small town, or in the country, potting soil can be found in stores. Compare the prices at chain stores, hardware stores, garden centers, and often even groceries. Your parents can help you figure out the "best buy" so your gardening money will go further.

It weighs less. The idea of container gardening is that the gardens can be moved around. Soil from your backyard or lot is heavy because it's packed down and filled with stones and rocks. You want your containers to be as light as possible so you don't need someone's help every time you want to move a potted garden.

It can be re-used. Although buying potting soil costs more than simply digging, you are able to use the soil over and over again for two to three years. You only need to throw soil away if plants are obviously diseased. When you start off right, it is easier to have success!

Plants

When shopping, keep a lookout for bargain plants. A sale table somewhere might have some plants you would like. Often, the plants are perfectly fine or just in need of a little fertilizer and a "haircut." Take care not to buy plants that might have insect or disease problems.

Sources

Most needed supplies should be available locally, from garden centers or chain or hardware stores. Other gardening materials might be obtained at botanic garden outlets or from gardening clubs, or purchased through the mail. Mail order catalogs are often packed with colorful photographs and provide all kinds of helpful information as well as offering a variety of plants and specialized gardening products. Look for suppliers in your local telephone listings or in gardening magazines.

Glossary

Annual—a plant that grows, flowers, produces seed, and dies all in one year

Backfill—to push soil back towards the base of plants to steady them

Belden basket—a hanging basket with many planting holes in the basket itself

Bonemeal—ground or crushed bone fertilizer good for growing bulbs

Clone—a plant that descends from a single ancestor

Crown—the part of a plant at soil level, between the root and stem

Cut flowers—those removed from plant for use in arrangement or displayed in vases

Cutting—a plant section (usually growing tip) that has been carefully removed to grow new roots

Deadhead—to remove dead or dying blossoms from a garden plant

Drainage—the process of allowing water to flow out

Flush—a spurt of plant growth, often referring to flowers

Force—a method of making a plant flower out of its natural blooming season

Frost-free date—average date for a particular area when outdoor temperatures are high enough that freezing does not occur

Germinate—when a seed sends out roots and shoots so the plant can grow

Hard frost—a thin layer of frozen vapor cold enough to kill annual plants

Herb—a plant grown for use in medicines, as food flavoring, or for its scent.

Inoculate—to implant microorganisms in an otherwise clean medium

Limestone—organic rock, made of shells, which when crushed is used to reduce acidity in soil

Market pack—a small plastic container, usually with four pockets, in which garden plants are often grown and sold

Mulch—sphagnum moss or other covering that helps prevent evaporation, protects the crown, and hides the soil line of plants

N-P-K—nitrogen, phosphorus, potassium: the major nutrients that plants need

Overgrown—too large or bushy for the container it is in (see Potbound)

Perennial—a plant that lives for more than two years. Perennials come up every year and produce flowers.

Pinch—use of fingers to remove growing plant tips to encourage bushy growth

Potbound—a plant in the same pot too long; may be overgrown and with roots wrapped too tightly to get nourishment

Precooling—a refrigeration process that prepares temperature-sensitive bulbs to start growing

Propagation—increasing the number of plants by various methods

Pruning—the trimming of plants to remove damaged or unwanted sections and encourage new growth

Repot—move a mature, growing plant into a different, usually larger, container

Seedling—also, plantlet; a baby plant with its earliest (seed) leaves

Spores—tiny seeds (as with mushrooms) that look like white dust

Sow—to sprinkle plant seeds

Staking—tying a plant to a stick or dowel to aid in support

Transplant—move a seedling or growing plant from one place to another

Vine—a plant with long flexible stems that can cling and climb

Water-in—to give a plant a good drink right after transplanting, and settle soil around its roots

Well rooted—when a plant's roots reach the bottom of its container

Wilt—the drooping downward of leaves and flowers

Index

annuals, 16, 17,
artificial lighting, 43

baskets as containers, 8, 51, 54
Belden baskets, 54
bulbs
    care after flowering, 35
    fertilizing, 32
    forcing, 30–31
    planting, 30, 32, 34
    selecting, 31, 33–34
    storing, 35
bushy growth, 7
butterflies, attracting, 17

cacti, growing, 28–29
cage, for tomato, 51–53
catnip toys, 37
colorful leaves, 11
containers, unusual
    bottle "pig," 56–58
    decorated cups, 40–42

planting stick, 55
    shoes, 36
    toys, 11–13
craft work, flowers for, 48
cuttings, 15

deodorizing plants, 37
dividing plants, 19, 24
drainage, 11–12
drying strawflowers, 48

edible flowers, 59–60
evergreen tree, decorating, 67

fertilize, when to, 9
fertilizer, 6, 32, 34
    strengths, 47
fertilizing
    herbs, 38
    tomatoes, 53

germination, 21

harvesting
    catnip, 37
    edibles, 60
    herbs, 38, 64
    lettuce, 55
    mushrooms, 27
    strawflowers, 48
    tomatoes, 53
herbs, 37–38
    in soil bag, 63
    use in cooking, 65
humidity, 43
    tent, building a, 27

insects, keep away, 37
ivy, 14–15

leaf cutting, plants for, 24
lettuce, varieties of, 54
limestone, 6

market packs, 5
miniatures, types of, 18

mulch, 10
mushrooms, growing, 26–27

names of plants, 68

overwatering, 12, 13

party decorations, 44–45, 49
perennials, 16, 17
plant ID and growing information,
    68–76
plant
    names, 68
    needs, 4
    size, 6, 15
planting stick, 55
plants
    butterfly-attracting, 17
    choosing, 5–6, 15
    insect-repelling, 37
    miniature, 18
    shopping for, 77
    staking, 6–7

pollination, 17
pot size, 15
propagation
    dividing plants, 24
    rooting a leaf, 22–23
    tip cutting, 24
pruning, 7, 19
    roots, 19

rooting
    leaf, 22–23
    tip cutting, 23

scent, strong, 31
"seed" leaves, 21
seedlings, 46–47
    fertilizing, 21
    transplanting, 22
seeds, starting, 20–22, 46
size, pot
    plant size equals, 6, 15
soil testing, 6

soil, 77
    calcium to "sweeten," 6
    healthy, 12
    potting, 6, 77
    seedling, 21
spores, 26
supplies, sources of, 77
support, providing, 6–7, 52
"sweeten soil," 6

tent, humidity, 27
time-telling container, 61–62
tip cutting, plants for, 24
tomatoes, growing, 51–53
tools, 5
toy as container, 11
transplanting, 14, 47
tree, evergreen, 66–67
tricking bulbs, 31

watering schedule, 10
wintering pansies, 50
work area, neat, 7

Acknowledgments

Thank you to all those who helped make this book possible:
Kyle, Christine, Jordan, Gus, Byron, Nicole, Monisha, Candace, Sandy,
Ruben and Cory—you were all a pleasure to work with. Thanks also
to their wonderful parents for letting them participate.
Carol (Mom) and Suzanne, for helping with all the setups.
Terry, Bruce T., and Cory, for being so patient.
Bruce Curtis, for introducing me to the world of publishing.
Caroline Kiang, for the use of some of your slides.

Sarah Mitchell Stika, for technical advice.
My thanks, too, go to the following businesses:
Agway (Riverhead Store); Bide-A-Wee Animal Shelter; Comstock, Ferre
& Co.; Friar's Head Farm; Green Island Distributors Inc.; Homeside
Florist; Ivy Acres, Long Island Cauliflower Association; Peconic River
Herb Farm; Phillip Schmitt & Son Farms Inc.; Suffolk County
Cooperative Extension; H. R. Talmage & Son; Trimbles of Corchaug